Contents

Where is Pakistan?

Here is a map of Pakistan.
Pakistan is a country in
South Asia.

Pakistan

Alice Harman

WAYLAND

Explore the world with **Popcorn** - your complete first non-fiction library.

Look out for more titles in the Popcorn range. All books have the same format of simple text and striking images. Text is carefully matched to the pictures to help readers to identify and understand key vocabulary.
www.waylandbooks.co.uk/popcorn

Published in paperback in 2014
Copyright © Wayland 2014

Wayland
Hachette Children's Books
338 Euston Road
London NWI 3BH

Wayland Australia
Level 17/207 Kent Street
Sydney NSW 2000

Produced for Wayland by
White-Thomson Publishing Ltd
www.wtpub.co.uk
+44 (0)843 208 7460

All rights reserved.
Editor: Alice Harman
Designer: Clare Nicholas
Picture researcher: Alice Harman
Series consultant: Kate Ruttle
Design concept: Paul Cherrill

British Library Cataloging in Publication Data
Harman, Alice. 1987-
   Pakistan. -- (Countries)(Popcorn)
   1. Pakistan--Juvenile literature.
   I. Title II. Series
   915.4'91-dc23

ISBN: 978 0 7502 8161 4

Wayland is a division of Hachette Children's Books,
an Hachette UK company.
www.hachette.co.uk

Printed and bound in Malaysia

10 9 8 7 6 5 4 3 2 1

Picture/Illustration Credits: Alamy: Picture Contact BV
13; Peter Bull 23; Stefan Chabluk: 4; Corbis: Alexandra
Boulat/VII 8, Mohsin Raza/Reuters 9, MK Chaudhry/epa 21;
Dreamstime.com: Dmitryp 7, Aprescindere 15 (and imprint),
Tommason 17(t); Photolibrary: Jim Holmes 11, Upperhall
Ltd/Robert Harding Travel 12; Shutterstock.com: Mina
Fouad 6, Pichugin Dmitry 10, Asianet-Pakistan 14, Takayuki
Hayato 16, Bonchan 17(m), Highviews 17(b), Naiyyer 18,
Asianet-Pakistan 19 (and title page), 20, Junker 22; Wikipedia:
Sgt1 Rik van Oijen 5.

Every effort has been made to clear copyright. Should there
be any inadvertent omission, please apply to the publisher
for rectification.

Islamabad is the capital of Pakistan. It is the ninth largest city in the country.

Around 1.7 million people live in Islamabad.

Faisal Mosque, in Islamabad, is the largest mosque in South Asia.

Land and sea

Some of the world's highest mountains are in the north of Pakistan. Further south, the land is flatter and there are large areas of forest and desert.

K2, in north Pakistan, is the second highest mountain in the world.

Saiful Maluk Lake is high in the mountains of northern Pakistan.

Pakistan has a short coastline, which is
in the south, along the Arabian Sea.
Karachi, the largest city in Pakistan,
is beside the coast.

People travel by boat from villages
on the coast to sell goods in Karachi.

The weather

Between March and May, it is hot and dry in most of Pakistan. There are sometimes droughts, when plants die and people don't have enough water to drink.

Hanna Lake, in the centre of Pakistan, dries out completely when there are long droughts.

The rainy season is from June to September. Storms and lots of rain can damage buildings and cause dangerous floods.

Donkeys are sometimes better than cars at getting through flooded city streets!

Town and country

Around half of the 182 million people in Pakistan now live in towns or cities. Cities are growing very quickly, and many people move from the countryside to find work.

Many cars, buses and trucks in Pakistan are decorated in bright colours.

There are lots of small farms
in Pakistan's countryside.
Farmers grow crops such
as chickpeas, rice and cotton.

Pakistan has nearly 50 million goats.
They are used for meat and milk.

Homes

Most houses in small villages are made from clay, stone and wood. Houses are normally on one floor only, with no stairs.

The Kalash tribe in north Pakistan build houses using stones and wood from the countryside.

12

Many people in Pakistan's cities live in small houses, often sharing a room. Some people live in flats in tall, new buildings.

More than 700,000 people live in Machar Colony, a crowded area of houses on the edge of Karachi.

 Shopping

There are large stores and new shopping centres in the cities. People also buy food, clothes and other goods at small shops and market stalls.

Factories make clothes in many colours and fabrics. They are sold in Pakistan and around the world.

Many people buy fresh fruit, vegetables and spices from street markets. Farmers often travel to markets to sell what they have grown.

In Pakistani villages, people often grow and sell small amounts of food.

15

 Food

Chapati is a kind of flat bread made from flour and water. People in Pakistan often eat chapati with their lunch and dinner.

Chapati is cooked on a flat griddle called a *tava*, over a small fire.

Paratha and naan are other popular types of bread eaten in Pakistan.

In the countryside, many families eat meals sitting on the floor around a knee-high table.

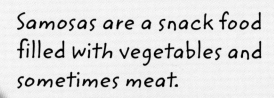

Samosas are a snack food filled with vegetables and sometimes meat.

Moong Dal curry is a popular and healthy dish of lentils cooked with spices.

Malai Khaja is a sweet pastry made with dried fruit.

 # Sport

Cricket is the most popular sport in Pakistan. The national men's cricket team has won many international competitions, including the World Cup.

Every year, the best cricket teams in Pakistan play for the Quaid-e-Azam Trophy.

Lots of people like to play and watch football. There are many football clubs around the country for men and women.

More than half of the world's footballs are made in Pakistan.

Children play football at school, and there are competitions between schools.

Holidays and festivals

Every year on 14 August, people across Pakistan celebrate the freedom of their country. Pakistan's Independence Day is a national holiday, so schools and offices are closed.

People watching Independence Day parades wave Pakistani flags.

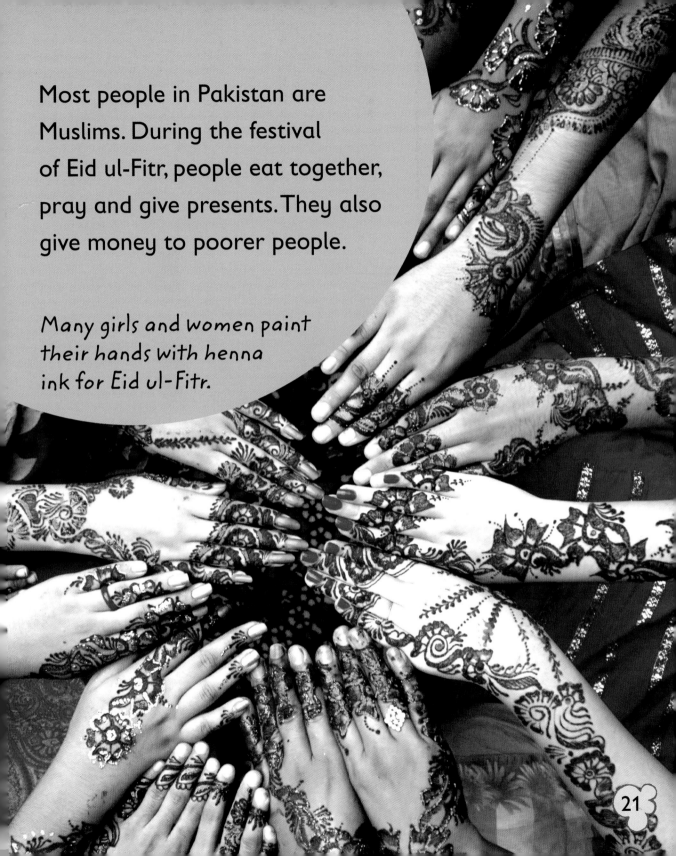

Most people in Pakistan are Muslims. During the festival of Eid ul-Fitr, people eat together, pray and give presents. They also give money to poorer people.

Many girls and women paint their hands with henna ink for Eid ul-Fitr.

21

Speak Urdu!

Many different languages are spoken in Pakistan. Urdu is Pakistan's national language. The sounds that make up some Urdu words are written below.

A-sa-lam o al-ay-kum	Hello
Jee harn	Yes
Jee na-heen	No
Ba-ra ay Me-her-ba-ni	Please
Shuk-ri-a	Thank you
Meer-a narm ... hay	My name is...
Koo-da ha-fiz	Goodbye

Green is a traditional colour for Muslims. The white line on the left stands for Pakistan's other religions.

Decorate a truck

You will need:
• scissors • glue • pen or pencil
• sheet of paper • coloured
tissue paper • glitter
• colouring pencils/pens/
crayons • sequins

Try to make your truck as colourful and fun as the picture on page 10 of this book!

1. Use your pen or pencil to copy this shape of a truck onto a sheet of paper. Draw the lines to show the windows, headlights and other features.

2. Cut out around the outside of the shape carefully, using the scissors.

3. Decorate your truck by drawing patterns with the coloured and gold and silver pens, by covering it with sequins and glitter, and by scrunching up and sticking on the tissue paper.

Glossary

capital the city where the government of the country meets

chickpea a round, pale brown seed that looks like a pea

clay a kind of wet earthy ground

cotton a light material, often used to make T-shirts

cricket a game where players hit a ball with a wooden bat

drought when there is little or no rain for a long time

fabric cloth from which things like clothes, curtains and sheets are made

flood when there is too much water because it has rained a lot

henna a red-brown paint that colours skin and hair

mosque a special building where Muslims meet to pray and worship God.

Muslim a person who believes in the religion of Islam

tribe a group of people that share the same language, culture and history

trophy an award given for winning or being good at something

Index

24